YOU ARE NOT LOST

poems by

Jeri Frederickson

Finishing Line Press
Georgetown, Kentucky

YOU ARE NOT LOST

Copyright © 2021 by Jeri Frederickson
ISBN 978-1-64662-577-2 First Edition
All rights reserved under International and Pan-American Copyright Conventions. No part of this book may be reproduced in any manner whatsoever without written permission from the publisher, except in the case of brief quotations embodied in critical articles and reviews.

ACKNOWLEDGMENTS

"The Moving Shelter" was first published in Thimble Literary Magazine Vol 3. No 1. Thank you to Editor Nadia Arioli and the team at Thimble for giving this poem a home.

Thank you, Finishing Line Press, for offering this manuscript a home out of the New Women's Voices chapbook contest.

Publisher: Leah Huete de Maines
Editor: Christen Kincaid
Cover Art: Jeri Frederickson
Author Photo: Jacqueline Jasperson
Cover Design: Elizabeth Maines McCleavy

Order online: www.finishinglinepress.com
also available on amazon.com

Author inquiries and mail orders:
Finishing Line Press
PO Box 1626
Georgetown, Kentucky 40324
USA

Table of Contents

I. Grow.

Arrested Development 1

Welcome at the Gates 2

The Poem in my Head 3

Summer Stock Night in the Berkshires 4

Penny Sized 5

The Moving Shelter 6

II. Pick.

Overripe Apples 11

III. Peel.

I Killed a Squirrel 21

How to Make a Snow Angel in Front of Your Lover 22

The Ex Who Still Emails Me 23

Turning my Childhood Kaleidoscope 24

IV. Core.

August: Central Park 27

Episode Two of *Our Planet* 28

Mourning the Tyger's Teeth 30

Rather than Failing 31

With Thanks 32

I.
Grow.

Arrested Development

This slide as an example of the past.
Press it down under a microscope.
Hazy. Clean it? It cries. It shakes.

She—the scientists think
the sample is a she—
stopped growing before she
could mature.

Please bring us another sample.

Welcome at the Gates

Have you come to Hell
in a fruit basket? Dying instead
to enter in a handbag? You're in luck!
We have designer bags

just one season out of date.
Would you like a peek?
Your future life
is free. No refunds.

Yes, your phone will be out
of range and will loudly ring.

The Poem in my Head

                        This is about you.

We can't publish this. So sorry but—

                    This poem is still trying to be about you.

Your fingers laced in mine
bursting the shared mitten.
I peered into your beard stubble
from my cracked contacts.

Let's dry this out so it's readable.

                    This poem is my hand.
                    You are beard stubble
                    in my contacts.

Summer Stock Night in the Berkshires

We search for light pulled
into all-consuming spirals.
You gaze more and speak

less with each search
for nebulas—a cluster
of death exhales lifetimes

into the solar system's muck
—the night brightens
as my bangs graze

your eyes. I inhale you
and tomorrow's acid. We stitch
together veins of gas and fire.

Penny Sized

I've spooked a lover twice and pretend no more.
They are like pretty bulbs in my lampstand.
They are career managers balancing yoga
at Machu Picchu and brunch on Sunday.

I've erased a penny memory.

You each felt like fifty bucks until it ended.
I would like to pretend I attract lovers
with decent credit lines
or without heroin as a hobby.

I've erased a nickel memory.

I become a hedge-fun-relationshipper.
In the sandbox we use
trucks and spoons to play pretend
cops and robbers. The winner gets
a shiny lampstand.

I've erased a quarter memory.
I've got four pennies left.

The Moving Shelter

The yellow cab driver looked back
when I said *I'm going
to get my ID and credit card,
then I want you to drive*

me home. Those quiet hands
turned the wheel toward me
as my friend's lip curled
and left the dark blood

on my chest. Halloween broke
into All Soul's. One hand on the wheel,
one rubbing his face, the driver
moved all the pieces of me

away from that curled lip,
those teeth with my blood.
His feet slowed the wheels
at every house I puzzled over.

*Not this one or that one,
but on this street* of light up ghosts.
I couldn't offer the truth: I'd only had
one drink the whole night.

He nodded as I opened
the car door. *I'm going
to come back, and then I want you
to take me home.* The driver

waited as I found my body
on the boards of someone's deck
and my ID with the host who asked if
I was okay and where my friend had

gone as I left to find the driver
waiting for my body to return
just as my ID returned
just as my credit card returned.

The whites of his eyes steadied
a road behind me as he drove me
to a home I couldn't lock the cold
out of. But for a while I was warm.

II.
Pick.

Overripe Apples
1920s-2021

Too many apples to care about one
knocked off by pickers competing to reach
the sweetest bite. Mom bargains for half price
a bushel for fallen ones, and we pull
the radio flyer through ruts to rows
of naked limbs. The full-price pickers eat
as they go and abandon their gnawed cores.
My family combs through their ghosts to glean
perfect fruit hidden among the bruised
wormy piles. Red peels stain our fingers
as I chuck the ones beyond redemption
down the row, not worrying about their
tomorrow—a single seed is worthless
unless that one uproots the whole damn tree.

Unless that one uproots the whole damn tree
an apple is worth less after falling
whether it released itself from the limb
or was knocked. *In the book of your life did
you mean to play the role of the second
other woman?* Mom asks. I've never plucked
an apple clinging to its branch. I've caught
one midfall, held it close, admired its gleam
until I twirled it around and found
squirming maggots in the core. How many
seeds is my life worth, and will I plant them
in time to grow? The ripped peel of my heart
curls into the ground as she presses me—
What can I do with you, my applesauce?

2012

What can I do with you? My applesauce
crank answers with a jolt, trying to hop
the counter's vice. Its spit candies my wrist.
I'm ten on this step-stool, pushing myself
and apples fresh from the flames down inside.
It is a hundred-and-eight-quart season.
When core and skin ooze from the side, the old
panting lab gets them—the one who'd let me
pluck out her lashes. Sugar, heat and sweat
turn the orchard's fallen rejects into
canned goods plopped into their baptismal bath.
One by one the seals bless us with a pop.
I hold a freshly filled jar—gurgling hot
begging for a new choice—I wring its neck.

1990s, 2000s

Begging for a new choice, I wring its neck
and plop the jar into the canning bath
scalding my fingers just like vacation
bible school seeded the red letters in
my ears. Like a cleansing fire, it grew.
Even now a freshly cracked bible spine
smells like steam from a hot apple pie. Mom
allowed one scoop of vanilla ice cream.
An omen. The night will meet its own woe.
My eyes burn as I taste last year's remains—

too sweet. Have we expired? Will the ribbed jars
seal their mark into my frozen fingers?
Can I toss the old, make a new choice? Or
am I left to this crank and steam again?

2000s

Am I left to this crank and steam again?
My job would've been cooking, but I'd sneak
out after Leroy. He was sent to get
you for lunch. Did you see the end ahead
of him as he ran toward the falling tree?
Did you see your brother's body? Were you
blamed? Did it sound like the peel of apple
skinned fresh between finger and knife? Did he
sizzle like the canning bath and pop his
lid? Did you boys sit still with mom for lunch?
Haven't we all yelled too quietly when
it was already late? Haven't we all
run the wrong way? I have. Will you tell me
or will I beg you again to see me?

1920s

Or will I beg you again to see me,
a child, in my best for the funeral,
soaking in silence, misunderstanding
like pesticide stunting a young blossom?
Or will rivers baptize empty orchards
where once I felt solitude but never

loneliness? I beg the trees and river
to grow a loving family without
harvesting their shame. Ancient seeds hush me
from their shriveled beds. Even now I am
kicking the ground open. *Grandmother, why
didn't you wait or tell me goodbye?* Could
she have tried to reply all these years? I
wouldn't have listened. It was the last time,
before her funeral, I chose to pray.

1999

Before her funeral I chose to pray
for another boat ride with grandmother
skiing slalom before my dad. I was
one of the kids with lifejacket buckles
flapping in the wind. Dad always squinted
at something I couldn't see, but I'd look
just as hard for it in the lake or lunch.
My tastebuds grew into her sugary
chunky applesauce. She wouldn't agree
with my life. I followed Dad's stare into
a rose and saw her casket underneath.
I am missing something he found. I pray
to the apples, the rose and that boat ride
to grow but never be called to bear fruit.

1990s

*To grow but never be called to bear fruit
is to fail at being a woman,* quip
the female leaders at a work lunch.
Am I in church again? Asked to recite
my life's purpose, nodding, choiceless like cores
planted for next spring. My skin is peeled back
between these women's knives. Am I allowed
to take up only the space my seeds need?
I am listening as the apple does
when leashed to the tree. Generations bear
down through my rigid core. A gooey mold
has overgrown unripened seeds. I'm pressed
to show them myself in public. What if
I am opened like an old cellar door?

2019

I am opened like an old cellar door.
Careful to follow every instruction,
I slice the apples. The wooden spoon stirs
up sweet juice, and the fluting starts. I am
spiced steam. I was clean, good, responsible,
evangelical. I chop pecans, peer
quietly under the sink. A bit bent,
the paint stirrer matches the wooden spoon.
Tools of parenting I outgrew. The pie
sizzles even as I tip the long knife
over and let it drip warm down my lips.
Mom outgrew the gluten, apple and pear

but still takes *just a smell, yum* as she leans
with a creaky spine and secrets below.

2010s

With a creaky spine and secrets below
its cover, the Bible sits at the table
of our holiday dinner, by the pie
lightly steaming its virtue into our bowed
heads. The slices baked into wholeness,
spices melting together like upper
to lower eyelids as the prayer starts.
The sticky apples beneath the crust's lid
glom onto the racing darkness my mind
invents like sins I might commit before
dessert. After some time, the prayer might
be over. I say amen and look up.
We are smiling, a final blessing:
the Lord will always provide enough food.

2016

The Lord will always provide enough food
and men to meet in chapel. The girls shoved
into clustered dorms each year. I smile
holding my wrench and mag light and wave them
through the chapel doors. The techies raise me
high in our unregulated Genie.
We are redeemed submerged in catwalk dust.
On break my parents ask *how is your soul?*
I hold a spoonful of peanut butter
in my mouth. I am lonely. *It is fine.*
The girls munch Braeburns and blush singing praise
for men who had no use for my life. Friends
ask years later *didn't you go with us?*
The juice will always be too sweet to drink.

2006-2010

The juice will always be too sweet to drink
freshly squeezed in Eve's red hands. Mom reached for
a purpose, found Abraham, Isaac and
Jacob's God like the tools of parenting
found her body. The father's word is law
and it is familiar—to find God
punishing through the fourth generation.
Mom finds her Adam, grafts to him. I grow
by His promise, unsure of my red hands.
Why are apples clinging to me? Must I
be this stained limb? We have seasons to grow.
The Lord God promised to water Mom's buds.

I plan a woe stronger than hope each time
we gather around the grace of crossed limbs.

Numbers 14:18

We gather around the grace of crossed limbs
and pluck each apple ready for harvest.
Mom said *Jonagold for baking, Braeburn
for eating, all for sharing* no matter
what. I pick three white peaches from their crate
and nestle each in soft tissue. Something
for me. She plucks out my favorite one.
I haven't had enough peaches this year.

I don't say yes for the first time but hand
her an apple. The orchard staff hovers.
My teeth unzip soft skin and the juice is
strangely bitter as it leaks down my lips.
If anyone else notices, I'll ask
they bless me as I'm falling from their tree.

2017

They bless me as I'm falling from their tree.
Their whispers—familiar bees and yellow
jackets—cover the insistent pruning
of preordained harvest. I'm removed and
I want to find home. I will become a
sapling, stretching my branches to starlings.
Someday I will uproot myself and search.
When I find my orchard, will they know me,
a piece of routine harvest? They are my
seeds' rigid shell, the crisp force of my peel
and the tartness in my juicy flesh. They
keep growing in me. Now I linger at
my orchard's open gates. What if there are
too many apples to care about one?

1998

Too many apples to care about one
unless that one uproots the whole damn tree.
What can I do with you? My applesauce
begging for a new choice—I wring its neck.
Am I left to this crank and steam again
or will I beg you again to see me
before her funeral? I chose to pray
to grow but never be called to bear fruit.
I am opened like an old cellar door
with a creaky spine and secrets below.

The Lord will always provide enough food;
the juice will always be too sweet to drink.
We gather around the grace of crossed limbs.
They bless me as I'm falling from their tree.

2021

III.
Peel.

I Killed a Squirrel

Its tail flapping
uncle uncle

the runner's dog barking
at the end of its leash

around and around
my bike wheels spin clean.

How to Make a Snow Angel in Front of Your Lover

Your beard is a worn bandage between my toes.
The hair on your arms chafes as it lulls me to sleep.

Your teeth flake my elbow. Cinnamon pours
your ribs onto blue green zeroes and ones.

In the patchwork of your room you make
the canvas, *Jeri, this is Rockford.* No. It's mud.

My voice sounds like the bottom layer of purple
when you want me. I made you wait. I won

by losing. 11 out of 10 would recommend again
the blistered cheek of freedom, the stunting

turpentine of goals. Float then. Roll shirtless in
sound waves. I will be whatever your *sturm und drang* is.

You will reach finally as finally I release the sleeping
dogs into trees, as purple deepens to a husky stop.

The Ex Who Still Emails Me
found poem in an unanswered, though definitely archived, email

Just wanted to say all of the hellos. Our last
convo's gone, if nothing else this will reach you and
I might ask how's life?! Or yawn, if nothing else.

An idea: my leftover coffee reached out and held your hand
once again. Yours is comfy – I mean life, and frankly I have
drawn a blank, if nothing else.

Every time I put the next day in the fridge
I'd love to hear all about your world. I haven't wanted
to say I think of you constantly, if nothing else.

Hello. Life is having a conversation, and I think of you. It's insane
and I'd undrink the koolaid. You feel like I only said if. Nothing else

I honestly throw as hard as I breathe. Tinfoil pipes off the stove have
no clue but still fold into your cheek. If nothing else

and hope button themselves together as the dress flying
behind your bike: you'll respond to this. Any reason you feel?
I hope you are nothing else

weird and dumb, tangled in the how, but so am I if nothing else.
I don't have to believe summer is gone. Just hey Jeri(!) if nothing else.

Turning my Childhood Kaleidoscope

In the mirrored end I see
        the puppy with a clown-carved face
        peeing as I come home
        whapping her soaked tail against the yellowing couch.

Safe for all ages.
        Do not hold up to the sun.

On the label:
        I am the girl who sat for hours
        over cooling coffee, breathing on the right
        words to soothe someone else's scrapes.

Turning I see a frog
        glowing against the rotting tree.
        A serpent ringed in red and black coils
        to strike. Growing out of the child's shoulder,
        the scales wrap through tissue in the ribs.
        Her shoulder is the forked tongue we never hear
        but in little wisps it tastes the air.

As it turns: I am the puppy
        sniffing a stone lady at the park
        draped in pigeon seasoning.

In the mirrored end
        I have set my childhood nightmares
        a place to rest their leather heads.

Turn and I am the snake. Turn and I am
        the frog. I will stick out my bright tongue
        to the snake. I will taste what I turn.

IV.
Core.

August: Central Park

The smell of pee and shit rises up the roped-off garden
as the city husks crawl through the park's branches
to goose the sky. My friend insists Manhattan
falls away, so I've wandered for hours

for this one spot where cicadas trill hidden
beside my sweaty path, where flies relieve
the itch between my sandals. The sparrows find
a place to land without plastic as they give witness

to the shells of rats run over by 1000 wheels an hour
on the path below me—the sound could reach the kittens
climbing over each other in tiny cages at the corner
as people hustle their thin mews as though my friend didn't

tell me he'd watched his dad drown a raccoon in a trash can
because the critter ate his bird's wing in the night
as it slept in its outdoor cage. We all become husks.
My friend tells me to go to Central Park—maybe

something there could allow me sight of the sky,
like I can burn brightly before these husks snuff out
everything by being there. Please let it be the sky.

Please pretend I'm getting air as they seal
my claws to their pissed streets and ask me
is it enough—*it is enough*—am I happy yet?

Episode Two of *Our Planet*

David Attenborough tells me / as the oil bubbles
in the pan / the walrus lost their ice.

The music cuts / I click the burner off and flip
the fish / silence as one hundred walrus fall

over each other in their thirst for water / I drop the fork / one hundred

sunburned giants tumbling over jagged rock where
ice used to be their slide / I lean

against the burner clicking but not lighting / as one hundred

times two tusks and flippers reach out / my face reaches for my fork /

the camera pans back / to tusks
embedded in the iceless ground. Bloodshot eyes

close / it is silent / it is silent / my parents called fish Walrus
food / to make me

eat my dinner / once a month we timed the Cincinnati zoo
visit with / the walrus feeding /

and I'd grab the bars / I grab a glass fill it
with whiskey and ice / bloodshot eyes

and a tusk as in the silence / I'm grabbing the bars /
the walrus were fed then sunbathed

in the zoo / and David Attenborough
tells me / above the silence / one hundred

walrus chose to avoid a stampede to relax
then // the ice melts // in my glass /

silence / then one hundred
walrus / in my glass asking for ice.

Mourning the Tyger's Teeth
after William Blake, for Greg

Tonight are you the crunching sound?
Are you my friend? I'm not ready to miss you.
When I said stay away were you around?
A lamb stains your paws, and you purr

as the forest snatches my wings.
Are you a friend? Your words launch spears
when I smile. My machete swings
and your stripes thicken the night.

When the burning sinews keep me warm won't you stay a friend?
Will you be a friend through the star-studded alarm?
Will you be a friend? Through the star-studded alarm
when the burning sinews keep me warm, won't you stay a friend?

And your stripes thicken the night
when I smile. My machete swings.
Are you a friend? Your words launch spears
as the forest snatches my wings.

A lamb stains your paws, and you purr.
When I said stay away were you around?
Are you my friend? I'm not ready to miss you.
Tonight are you the crunching sound?

Rather than Failing

We pick apart the discord in the front pew
as the singers fight each other's notes. We roll
our eyes at the worship leader's new goatee.
We yell at the driver blowing the red light as we turn left.

We argue over what is actually gluten
and soy free at Panera. We pick apart each other's
attempts to train the dog to stay or be soothed
during storms. We take turns calling her over

to rub her belly and scratch her left ear. We watch
her tail flit above the tall grasses she circles
as the squirrels she never catches chatter.

Let us talk of the amount of rain that's fallen
or the potholes in the road or anything but
the question we have for each other. Of parenthood

and childhood. I am grown, you are going deaf.
We love each other. Let us take the dog for a walk.

WITH THANKS

I wish to acknowledge and thank the generous mentorship of the faculty at Antioch who saw early and mid versions of these poems. Specifically, thank you to Maggie Smith, Colette Freedman, Jim Daniels, Richard Garcia, Xochitl-Julisa Bermejo, Carol Potter, and Victoria Chang for encouraging and challenging me, one poem at a time, to gain an understanding of the depth and complexities of poetry.

Thank you to Dr. Rhoda Burton for opening my eyes to formal poetry over a decade ago and to Pablo Peschiera for returning delight to poetry as I finished my senior year at Hope College.

Thanks and cheers to my fellow writers at Study Hall Workshops, Women Who Submit and the Chicago chapter, especially for all the weeks gathering online rather than in person due to Covid. Thank you Awakenings and the survivor community for constantly showing me new ways of healing and creating and for breaking taboos.

My eternal gratitude to my cohort at Antioch University Los Angeles (go Cardinals!). Mick, Patrick, Janet, and Leo, your writing, your feedback, and our conversations made a deep impact on me. Loumarie, thank you for interviewing me on Lunch Ticket and pushing me to talk about my own work.

Thank you to my longtime friends for supporting me, and specifically to Eileen for the long cemetery walks. Thank you, Jess and Michael, for attending my poetry readings and for the honest "I don't know what that was about, but I'm here for it and you." Thank you, Megan, for listening for years before any of this was written. Thank you, Lacey, for waking up early every week for years to talk to me from across the Pacific, and for buying and reading every journal my work has been published in for over a decade.

Most importantly: Thank you to my family who shows love in many ways even through the fear of having a writer in the family.

Thank you, reader, for opening this chapbook.

Jeri Frederickson calls Chicago home with her two cats and many plants. She swims in literary, visual, and performing arts as an expression of survival. She writes, edits, directs, and curates as a channel to nurture love and access beauty while questioning the experiences that hold people together.

She graduated from Antioch University Los Angeles with an MFA in Writing and from Hope College with a BA in Theater and English. She is the Creative Director of a nonprofit arts organization whose mission centers survivors of sexual violence. In the Chicago theater community, she is a member of Irish Theatre of Chicago, and spent ten years as a stage manager. Jeri has been published in print and online in *Vine Leaves, Thank you for Swallowing, Awakened Voices, Thought Collection,* and *Thimble Literary Magazine.* You can find her @bshl_furmonsters and jericreatesthings[at]gmail.com

www.ingramcontent.com/pod-product-compliance
Lightning Source LLC
LaVergne TN
LVHW041505070426
835507LV00012B/1339